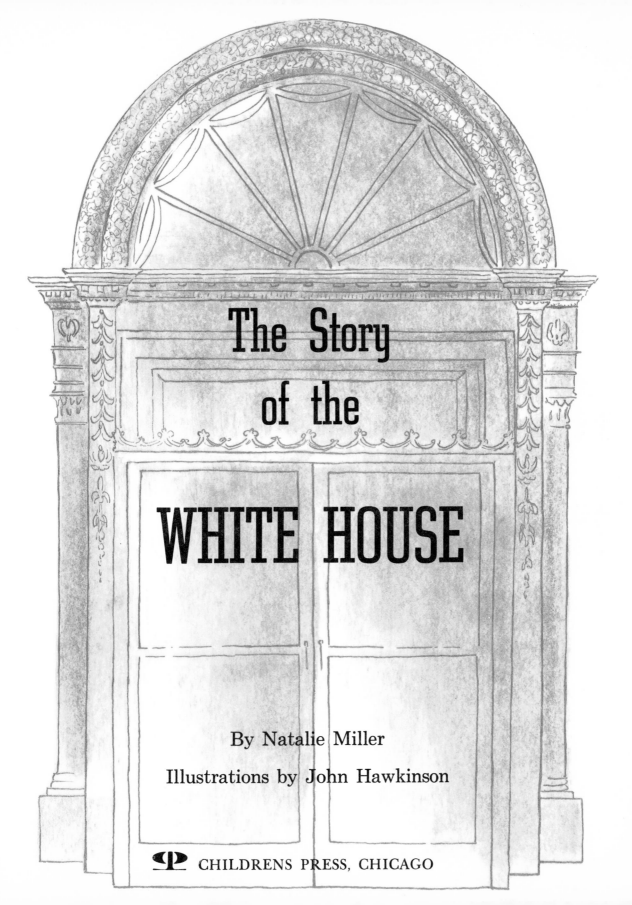

The Story
of the
WHITE HOUSE

By Natalie Miller

Illustrations by John Hawkinson

CHILDRENS PRESS, CHICAGO

Library of Congress Catalog Card Number: AC 66-10305

15 16 17 18 19 20 21 22 23 24 25   R   75 74 73

James Hoban hurried into the kitchen. His wife was ladling stew from the big kettle hanging in the fireplace.

"I can earn $500, and help our country at the same time," he said waving a newspaper. "Do you remember last year when Congress was looking for a permanent home for the federal government?"

Mrs. Hoban nodded. "They decided to build a special city for it along the Potomac River, right in the center of the thirteen states," she said.

"Well, the commissioners planning that city offer a prize of $500 to the architect who can design the best house for the President," he explained. "I think I can do it."

"What kind of a mansion do you have in mind?" asked Mrs. Hoban as she set the bowls of stew on the pine table.

"It must be gracious," he began. "But not so elegant that the President will think he is a king. It must be fine enough to entertain foreign diplomats. It must be a very special house—one that will have a life of its own and can grow with the country."

5

After supper Mr. Hoban put all his architecture books on the kitchen table. He was so absorbed in them he didn't notice when Mrs. Hoban quietly left to go to bed.

For weeks he thought of nothing but the mansion. When his plans were finished he sent them by stage-coach to the commissioners.

Eighteen other architects sent plans, too, and the judges studied each one carefully. At last they chose Mr. Hoban's and took the drawings to President George Washington for his approval.

It was Washington's dream that the new little country should some day have the most beautiful capital city in the world. He had ridden his great horse along the Potomac and personally picked out the exact ten square miles for the Federal City at Congress' request. He had appointed Major Pierre Charles L'Enfant to design the city and select the sites of the important buildings.

Washington laid Mr. Hoban's drawings on his desk. He studied them with great care. He knew from experience how important it was for the President to have a proper residence.

"You have made a good choice, gentlemen," he said. "That oval room will be fine for greeting distinguished visitors, and that great East Room is excellent for formal receptions and dances."

"Thank you, Mr. President," one of the men said. "But we thought we would ask Mr. Hoban to make the rooms smaller to save expense. Our little country does not need such large rooms in its President's home.

Washington frowned angrily. "Our country will grow and the residence of the first citizen must be able to grow with it," he said earnestly. "Omit the porch and wings if necessary, but do not cut down on the size of the rooms."

So in July of 1792 the commissioners invited James
Hoban to come to the Federal City (later called
Washington, D.C.) to supervise the building of the
house without its porch and wings.

When Hoban arrived from Charleston, South Caro-
lina, he found the "city" a wilderness of swampy
land and mud with only a few scattered houses, but
he was not dismayed.

On October 12, 1792 the cornerstone for the President's mansion was laid. It was the first government building started in the Federal City.

"The government doesn't plan to move here from Philadelphia until 1800," thought Hoban happily. "Surely in eight years I can build a fine mansion. There may even be enough money for porches by that time."

But Congress was slow in granting money. Workmen did not like to stay in the swampy land filled with mosquitoes. Materials were hard to get.

President John Adams and his wife Abigail were ready to move in, and there were only six rooms finished!

Abigail Adams arrived on the night of November 16, 1800. Her coach had been lost in the woods and she was cold and tired.

The President had arrived two weeks earlier and was there to greet her and show her around the new house. The rooms seemed to her like enormous caves in the candlelight.

Great fires burned in the fireplaces but Abigail felt chilly as soon as she moved away from them.

"The plaster is still damp," the President explained.

"I would like some hot tea to warm me," she said. "Would you ring for the servant?"

"There are no bells in the house yet," he told her, "but I already have instructed a servant to bring some. I have also ordered plenty of water for you to wash after your trip. Water has to be carried a half mile and sometimes there is a delay."

Her husband explained that the ground floor was for the work rooms and the servant's quarters. The first floor was for the official state rooms and the second floor was for the family, with one room set aside as the President's office.

Abigail was pleased when she went up the unfinished stairs and saw that her own crimson furniture had arrived and been placed in her oval sitting room.

The next morning Abigail looked out at the sea of mud around the mansion. There were workmen's huts scattered about and kilns close by. When there was laundry to be hung she wisely decided to hang it in the unfinished East Room.

There were many inconveniences but Abigail could imagine what it would be like someday. She wrote her daughter, "This House is built for ages to come" and it is more true with each passing year.

To lend dignity to the structure, President Adams decided to call it the President's Palace. The country was growing. The capitol was being built. Nine men were working in the Post Office on 9th Street. Six employees of the State Department shared the rooms of the Treasury Department on New York Avenue.

On New Year's Day, 1801, the Adams' held the first formal reception in Abigail's upstairs oval room. The Marine Band in bright red coats played softly. Fires glowed and candles twinkled. President Adams bowed deeply to his guests as he had seen it done in European palaces.

Three months later, Thomas Jefferson became President. Since the mansion is occupied only by the man in office, the Adams' moved out and Jefferson moved in.

He did not think that the President of all the people should live in a "palace." He called his home the "President's House."

Jefferson claimed the big stone house was big enough for "two emperors, one Pope and the Grand Lama." But he took great delight in finishing and furnishing many of the rooms and adding a porch and low colonnades.

He furnished the state oval room quite elegantly and used it to meet important dignitaries, as Washington had suggested. Since then all the other presidents have used it for the same purpose and it is the most beautifully furnished room in the whole house. It is called the Blue Room today.

Jefferson did not bother to finish the great East Room. He used it as an extra pantry and did his formal entertaining in the two parlors on either side of the Blue Room. Because of the colors used, they are called the Red Room and the Green Room today.

President Jefferson loved parties and invited all kinds of people. There were Indian Chiefs in war bonnets. There were foreign dignitaries with gold coats and slippers with curled-up toes. There were common workmen in homespuns.

Jefferson was interested in the capital city, too. Pennsylvania Avenue was a bog. He made it fit for carriages and planted poplar trees along it.

The next President was James Madison, who had a wife named Dolly. She had many gay parties in the President's House.

When Congress granted some money for furniture, Dolly bought mirrors to brighten up the house.

One time she invited all the children in Washington to an Easter egg roll on the lawn. She dyed hundreds of eggs herself so that there would be enough. Everyone had fun.

In 1814 the United States was at war with England. President Madison was away when word came that the British were marching on Washington.

Dolly carefully packed important state papers and sent them away. As the British were entering the city, she ordered a large picture of George Washington, who had been her husband's close friend, to be taken from the frame and hidden.

Then Dolly, disguised as a poor farmer's wife, entered a waiting coach and fled to safety.

That night the British burned all the government buildings in Washington. The next day all that was left of the President's House were the four blackened outside walls.

Mr. Hoban was asked to come back and rebuild the mansion using his original plans.

When it was ready, and the blackened walls had been painted white, James Monroe, was President.

It had cost so much to rebuild the house, Congress had very little money left for furniture. President Monroe offered to sell some of his own beautiful French furniture to the government for far less than he had paid for it. With the rest of the money Congress had allotted, he ordered some special pieces from France. Some of them are still used in the mansion today.

The Monroe's liked to live in a formal way. They used gold spoons and forks for state dinners. When the people heard about it they did not like it. Gold spoons were for kings, they said. And who ever heard of using forks! Knives were good enough for Americans!

Monroe felt that the title President's House was not elegant enough, so he had the name officially changed to Executive Mansion. But because it was a gleaming white, the people called it affectionately the White House.

Andrew Jackson was the first President to be born in a log cabin. Backwoodsmen and common people felt that he was one of them and so they came to his inaugural reception in 1829.

They crowded into the house, stood on the brocade chairs to get a better look at their hero. They broke many glasses. It was the rowdiest reception the White House has ever seen.

Just before he left office, Jackson was given a huge cheese weighing 1400 pounds! He invited anyone to come who wished to help him eat it on Washington's Birthday. Before the day was over the cheese was smeared everywhere. It was weeks before the White House was clean again.

Three important things happened to the mansion while Jackson was President.

Water was piped into the building. It no longer had to be carried in by buckets.

A north porch, called a portico, was added. This gave the White House its address of 1600 Pennsylvania Avenue.

"This entrance shall be used only by kings and queens and very important people," Jackson announced. His order still holds today.

The third thing was the completion of the East Room—thirty years after Abigail Adams had hung her laundry there.

It became the formal reception room that Washington had expected it to be. But it also has been used for many things Washington had not imagined.

Many of the children who have lived in the White House have found it just the place for roller skating, stilt-walking, bicycle riding and racing games.

Tad Lincoln raced his goats in there but had to stop during the Civil War. Beds for Union troops filled the room.

President John Quincy Adams kept a live alligator there for a house guest and President Teddy Roosevelt found it made a good place for exercising and wrestling.

Gradually the eighteen acres around the mansion were drained and gardens planted. The house and the grounds were constantly changing, reflecting the mood of the country and the family who lived there.

When new forward-looking inventions came along, the President's home was often one of the first to use them.

Gas lights came on the market in the 1840's and were installed in the White House.

"Candlelight is so pretty can't we at least leave candles in the big chandelier in the East Room?" pleaded President James Polk's wife.

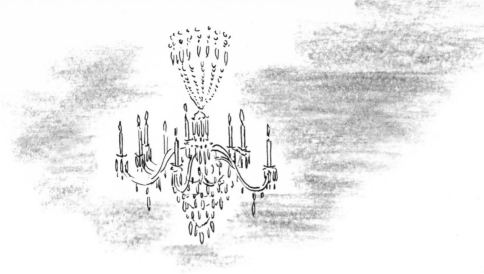

To please her, the candles remained. At a big party when all the lights were turned on at one time, the gas failed. Mrs. Polk's candles were the only lights in the whole house. Everyone was glad she had insisted that they stay.

In 1850 President Fillmore made headlines when he had a bathtub put in the White House. People worried about him. Tub bathing was considered dangerous. When Fillmore stayed well all during the winter, people decided maybe the tub was all right.

Fillmore also bought a cookstove for the kitchen, but his cook refused to use it.

"I cook very well on this big fireplace. I cook banquets for kings on this fireplace. I see no need to change," said the cook stubbornly. "Anyway, I don't know how to work all those fancy drafts and things."

President Fillmore went to the patent office and studied the plans for the stove. He learned to work the drafts and taught the cook how to use the stove.

While her husband was helping the cook, Mrs. Fillmore, who had been a teacher, realized that the White House had no books—not even a dictionary! Quickly Congress granted money for a White House library and Mrs. Fillmore was happy to choose the books for it.

All the families who have lived in the mansion have had their own ideas on how it should be decorated while they were there.

When dapper Chester Arthur became President, he refused to move in until the whole place was redecorated and refurnished. He had twenty-four wagonloads of furniture hauled away and sold at auction.

Today he could not do that for there is a law that all unwanted White House furniture must go to the Smithsonian Institution.

As the country grew, so did the mansion. Telephones were installed. Electricity took the place of gas.

The President's office on the second floor spilled over into several rooms until the families were squeezed into smaller quarters. When the Prince of Wales was visiting, President James Buchanan gave the Prince his room and slept in the hall!

When Theodore Roosevelt and his large family moved into the White House in 1901 there were only six rooms left for them. The President's growing staff and cabinet had taken over thirteen rooms.

"Something has to be done at once," said the vigorous young President. "This house is much too small, and the engineers tell me the foundations are weak."

Congress agreed that the 100-year-old house needed a good renovation. The Roosevelts moved out and painters, engineers and carpenters swarmed all over it.

They put steel beams in the basement and enlarged the dining room to seat a hundred people at one time. They added a wing for the President's offices, and for the first time the second floor became a private family home.

"Let's change the name officially to the White House," Roosevelt said to Congress. "That's what everyone calls it anyway."

So in 1902 Congress passed a law making the official title the White House.

When work on the house was completed, the whole country was proud of how fine it looked. But in another twenty-five years the country had grown so much the house seemed too small again.

Since a new roof was needed, President Calvin Coolidge had a third floor added with extra bedrooms and storage space.

In the 1930's President Franklin Roosevelt had a swimming pool added.

During World War II blackout curtains were hung at the windows so that no light could escape, and machine guns were mounted on the roof. Extra offices and a bomb shelter were built underground.

After the war, in 1948, when President Harry Truman was shaking hands with a long line of people in the East Room, he heard a strange cracking sound. The great chandelier began to rock. He kept right on shaking hands but the next morning he called in engineers to inspect the house.

Their reports were alarming. The foundations had been riddled with pipes and wires for all the new inventions and additions over the years. It had become the most famous house in the country and hundreds of sightseers went through every day the tours ran. The poor building was under a great strain and might collapse at any time!

The Trumans moved out and the country had to think about what to do with this very special house.

Some young architects suggested tearing down the old house and building a modern one. Suddenly the American people realized how much the old mansion meant to them. The spirit of America was held within these riddled walls. They loved the house and did not want it changed.

At last it was decided to dismantle the rooms, piece by piece, and use everything possible in a rebuilt house.

Skilled workmen took down the doors, the panels, the moldings—everything that could be saved or used as a model to copy. They took pictures, made drawings and tagged each piece so they would know exactly where it should go.

Then workmen with bulldozers cleared out the whole inside. Only the four walls were left standing as they had been after the fire in 1814.

Within the walls, workmen built two floors underground and four floors above ground on a strong foundation that could stand an enormous amount of strain. The basic plans the architects used were the ones drawn in 1792 by James Hoban. This time the house was built, there was no problem about money. Congress gladly paid the bill of nearly six million dollars and workmen were proud to have a chance to work on the beloved building. People all over the world watched the progress of the restoration with interest and read about it in their newspapers.

In 1961 Mrs. John Kennedy, seeing how proud the American people were of their White House, revived and expanded a project to restore the furnishings that had been used in the mansion.

Generous citizens have donated antiques that belonged to former presidents or are authentic pieces of other eras. It has helped to make the White House a showcase of the country's past.

More than a million people take the sight-seeing tour each year through the state rooms, beginning in the ground floor corridor where Mrs. Woodrow Wilson learned to ride a bicycle when no one was looking. They are thrilled to see the many things that are links with the past—the portrait of George Washington that Dolly Madison saved, the dining table centerpiece that Monroe ordered from France, the gold and white East Room where royalty has danced.

James Hoban planned a mansion that would grow with the country. George Washington recognized the beauty of his plans and saw that they were not changed. Abigail Adams visualized its future when she said it was a house built for ages to come.

Each President added something to the life of the mansion. The house that took so long to build and that has seen the country grow from a poor and weak Republic to a rich and powerful nation tells the story of that growth in living history. It is a most beautiful and beloved landmark and one of the most famous houses in the world.